Eat The Peach

A Collection of Poems
by Nick Pemberton

with an introduction by Emma McGordon

Published by Tutti Frutti Press 2021
tuttifruttipress@gmail.com

Cover artwork and logo by Carlo Castelvecchi,
design by Francesca Halfacree.

Printed and bound in Great Britain by
Clays Ltd. Elcograf S.pA

For Jack, Sam,
Tom & Lily Pemberton.

Acknowledgements

Thanks to Jack, Sam, Tom & Lily Pemberton for giving their permission to publish these poems.
Becca Roberts for her keen proofreader's eye.
Brindley Hallam Dennis, Darren Harper & Owain Lewis for reading through.

Previously, "Three Sides Of The Moon" was in *The Barrovian* in 1965.
"Where Eden Flows," "English Ghost Dance" & others were in *Art, Medicine, Life, Death Work and the Whole Ball of Wax*, published by Selkirk Lapwing Press in 2006.
"He Went Down To The Weir This Morning" was in *An Accessible Paradise* in 2007.
"Dad's End Of The Deal" was in *Beautiful Scruffiness* in 2010.
"Word From The Island" won second place in The Portico Poetry Prize in 2013.
"Once Upon A Time In Cumberland" & "Carlisle - Summer - Foot & Mouth" were in *Fires In The North* in 2014.
"Border City" was in *Poetrybay* in 2016.
"The Transparency of Shadows" was in *100 Vapour Trails* published by Hedgehog Press in 2018.
"First Meeting" was first published in *Acumen*.
"Footprints," "Morning In Andalucía," "Neighbours," "Possible Futures 70," "Learning To Look," "Pictures Of The Gypsy Kids," "Poem For George Tod" & "Drunk In The Country" were in *Ambit*.
"Sleight Of Hand," "Drunk In The Country," "The Colours Of Birds," "Low Tide" & "Highway Child" were in *Envoi*.
"Lines For A Doctor On Retirement" was in *Other Poetry*.
"Typewritten Poem To My Bank Manager" & "Sonnet For MacSweeney" were in *Penniless Press*.
The English Reservation was published somewhere, but we can't remember where…

Nick Pemberton was a writer since he could write words down. His first published work was a poem about the moon in a school magazine when he was thirteen.

Sent mad by this early success, he wrote TV annuals, comic strips, paperback novels, plays for stage and radio, short stories, and the odd column for national newspapers.

He also stripped furniture, worked in a circus in Spain and taught Creative Writing at the University of Cumbria.

Between times he tried to write a couple more poems.

Editor's note.

It has been a pleasure, a privilege & quite a lot of work to get this publication together. I knew Nick for at least 14 years, though our paths had crossed before then.
I was with him when he wrote many of these, & heard him read most of them aloud. Sometimes he would ask me my opinion on a poem, a work in progress. It would be hard to know what to say, as who knew what was going on in that head of his..?
Usually, if he had to read it to me, it wasn't quite finished. (When is a poem finished?)
If he was kinda happy with it, he'd keep it to himself.
After he died I discovered a folder he'd kept called "Poems For A Collection."
Aha! So those were ones he thought were keepers! Although he wrote a lot more, I decided to stick to those but took the liberty of adding his first published poem - "Three Sides Of The Moon," & his last - "The Transparency Of Shadows," which I know he was pleased with.
Although many of these have been published elsewhere, he never got them together in one collection.
With just a bit of tweaking, & some help, I think we've managed to do his work justice.
I hope you will enjoy reading them, & reading them again, & think of him whenever you watch the turn of the tide...

Francesca Halfacree, Carlisle 2021.

Introduction.

I first met Nick at an open mic night in Cockermouth, Neo's Gallery, just over the bridge, in a place that is now a bike shop. I'd heard of Nick through a mutual friend - Barry MacSweeney - one of the many figures you will find among these pages. I too had experienced the "slurred, milky phoneline" at 4am. And so we were connected through the telephone wires of drunken Far Northern Poets. At the end of the night Nick invited me to start teaching at the University of Cumbria where he was course leader. For two years I had the pleasure of sharing a coffee with him once a week after the class. And so now, reading these poems, I hear his familiar voice but also feel invited into a less familiar territory, one that I believe comes only with posthumously published work - I feel led by an invisible hand. These poems offer reflective meditations, sometimes written on scraps, by a man wandering through the mystery of the world with all its discombobulated fragments - finally accepting the senselessness of reason. Perhaps the sense of acceptance comes only because we know Nick is no longer with us, because the poems themselves are filled with a search that, at times, seems Lear-like - the man gone mad ranting on the heath - he did rant - his performances were rant-like and filled with tender moments. Among the most tender in this collection, Dad's End of the Deal, a poem whose lines themselves, "accelerated / forkings of the myriad roads of possibility," are thick with meaning and yet manage to avoid sentimentality through wry humour and a directness that can only be described as love itself.
Many of the most personal poems feel muscular in their syntax, especially the poems for his brother. There are also monolithic retellings of myth with the weaving in of fact and fiction, placing heroes, or in many cases, anti-heroes, in the rural surrounds of Northern England. I urge you to give these poems the time they need to be read, re-read and absorbed as the story-teller requires.

Nick's sharp dry humour is ever-present as is his idea of himself as one in a long line of outcasts somewhat misunderstood. In Typewritten Poem to My Bank Manager he signs himself off as "The Ghost of Tom Joad," a reference to both Springsteen and Steinbeck, and also quotes throughout Dylan, Blake, Milton and the lesser-known Leadbelly, who did time for a debt he did not owe. It is intertextually rich, culturally aware and once again echoes MacSweeney, placing Nick, like Barry, in a generation of men full of the promised freedoms of the 60s and yet confusingly constrained by a modern world of hashtags and crypto-currencies. And so nature and existentialism become the paths that lead to greater freedoms. A lake, "surface as dark as an x-ray," offers a way that, by observing ourselves in the outside nature that we are inextricably a part of, we get glimpses of that which is inside, that which is below our own surface. The depths of the poems are balanced by Nick's eye for the sublime within the banal and the sheer ridiculousness of being human - a family photograph album that "every few pages / amongst workmates and family / were photos of fish. / Hundreds and hundreds of them."

It is a very funny collection. Nick was a funny man and a great believer in the power of words, stories and community. He was a dedicated encourager of other writers and I count myself lucky to be one of those writers who was touched by his generosity of spirit. I heard of his death through the wires of Cumbrian gossip. I'd not seen him for a number of years though we would exchange irregular Facebook messages and comments. I didn't know he was ill, so it came as somewhat of a shock. There is comfort in these poems for the ones who are left to continue that, at times, make it sound like he had it all worked out, as he tells us "Love, lose, solve, evolve," but then he reminds us of the fragility of it all, concluding that "each life is a shout on the earth / beneath the tree that gives us shelter."
It's a great collection, one that deserves to be read and re-read, it's a world within a world to lose yourself in, and hopefully come out knowing something more of the question though definitely not the ever-elusive shape shifting answer.

Emma McGordon, London 2021

CONTENTS

Moon

Tides

Islands

Flight

Moon

three sides of the moon

The bitter moon is tall in the sky
And the stars blink frostily as
My footsteps slap at the midnight silence.
Tonight I am aware of the moon
And I see that its curve,
Although caught upon the vague parabola of infinity,
Is concise, a crystal of reality,
Giving this point on the infinite curve of existence
The clarity, the nearness and the honesty
Of a knife edge.

So in our lives,
When for a distillation of a moment, we know ourselves;
When we leave the curve of time
As it arches downward to senility,
And we see ourselves mirrored in the clarity of the moment.
Like the moon, our image is naked and honest,
Filled with the knowledge that these stolen moments
Are our only contact with the infinite.
But the moon maintains its touch;
While we, in our fearful eagerness, fumble our moment.

the story of my life (to be read very very very fast)

Come here
do this
watch that
count those
go there
feel this
think that
try these
dry those

never ever let them know
never ever let it show

hate this
love that
keep it fat
keep it thin
let it out
keep it in
yaketty yak
take the flak
go away then come back

Come back go away
come back go away
All of this is throwaway
come back go away
go go go go go go go go go
going going glowing flowing
bridge is burning wind is blowing
snow across the cinders in my heart

hear it hiss hear it smoulder
every second growing older
older colder never bolder
growing growing going

flowing going
going flowing
going
going
going
going
absolutely nothing left...   ...it's gone

picture book

Here's a book, a picture book,
with pictures of poets that shows to us
a single moment in a day, frozen fast in a book that says:

here's a book, a picture book,
stuffed with dreams and love and stuff,
with pictures and poems that show to us
men and women who've had enough
of a single moment in a day, frozen fast in a book that says
that - for this moment - there is only this:

- just this book, this picture book,
just one more book, like other books all
stuffed with dreams and love and stuff,
so take it down and take a look.
This old broken book will show to us
- torn jacket, cracked spine, its corners scuffed -
men and women who've had enough
and grown weary of picturing a picture of a picture
of a single moment in a day, frozen fast in a book that says
(like water on a pebble that the sunlight will erase)
that in this life there's only this:
the imprint of a lover's kiss.

Here's a book, a picture book,
a magic book, although it looks
just one more book, like other books all
slumped in ragged rows on shelves
stuffed with dreams and love...and stuff
that skips like the moon on the water between us.
So take it down and take a close hard look
and listen too, to all that moves within this book.
This book of pictures, of poems, of poets still speaks to us
- torn jacket, cracked spine, its corners scuffed -
still takes us to another place, a shared time full
of men and women who've had enough

4

wit and sense not to simply dream of dreaming
or picturing a picture of a picture of a picture.
They - no we - are true dreamers.
We dream the present, not the past,
not just a single moment in a day,
frozen fast in a book that says
that this moment is all there is.
Instead, they work and hope and wish
that - like water on a pebble - the sunlight will erase
the stain that spreads through all our days,
for in this life there's only this:

every day's slow falling, like snow falling softly as
the imprint of a lover's kiss.
The book is closed. It was not much.
The book is closed. The pages touch.

a hippie too long in rural surrounds

Though now it is winter, come visit me.
Come walk the bleak walk to my door and knock.
Wait while I draw back the bolts and unlock
my natural habitat. Welcome.
Grab a seat by the window, look at the view.
True, nothing changes. The place is a dump
and the spring is broken and can't be mended.
Don't be offended, but both puns intended.

Push papers aside, bottles too,
- care for a plate of yesterday's stew? -
the past's always with us but can't be fixed
when all's said and done. Here let me pour
you just the one. And some for the blokes
who blink at my jokes. You have me sussed
already, I suppose, as just one more
difficult, timewarped, cranky bore.
A sad wanker waging low-level war
on the landed, loaded, four-wheel driven
local folk who run things round here and who,
to be honest, are too preoccupied
with slicing up the sticks and countryside
like a carvery roast to even notice...

- (The carvery's Ye Olde Greene Man, by the way,
part of a chain. Their motto: The more you eat,
the less you pay. Have a nice day.) -

...while amongst pink dead hills of spotless meat
and car parks packed with gleaming new estates,
in an empty garden, gangster starlings
squabble round crisp packets and rose petals
and Saturday's glasses fill with Sunday's rain...

Sorry. The mind tends to wander nowadays.
Focus is shot. Clarity too. Resolve squandered.

One more bleeding heart with redneck tastes
and weakening resistance; - that's yours truly.
And that stranger staring from the mirror
- could it be? That gaunt, haunted guy -
is that me, holed up in the back brain
hiding from hunters? Sometimes he watches
me while I stubbornly, pointlessly polish
these old medals from failed campaigns
to save whatever it was; - the whale,
the planet, society from itself,
the best till last, each other from pain...   I forget...

Please. No. Don't go. One more tot and a toast.
To our children's children and their kids' kids.
Whether they inherit this place or not,
may they know it - not as a place where
you pay for a signed copy of the view
- but as home.

I mean it, man. Peace.

drunk in the country

Wandering through bracken and boulders in search
of a river whose track he lost long ago,
drunk as a skunk in summer's fecund fields,
he thought: to be born and feel the sky,
bright & silver, pierce your eye is enough

but among thistle, sandstone and sudden moss,
his feet failed him and he foundered. Gravity
tugged glass from his hand. Land leaped up to smash it.

What is changeless in the world,
said a voice inside him - like water on rock
scoured and pitted by the clear stream -
gives rise to dreams and shapes of dreams
towards which our blind lives reach and stumble.

"Wrong," buzzed a wasp, a fine-waisted dandy
stepping in striped jacket through the sweet
lost treasure that scented the broken shards
scattered before his face as he lay there,

"a world such as you have imagined,
a chaotic geometry of elided signs,
immutable laughter and echoed cries,
you would find unbearable."

His lids grew heavy.
His eyes closed against the sky's aching light.
The silent, remembered river flowed on, unseen.

storm warning

At the conference on pooling best practice
they are talking about mental health.
The woman in the flowered patterned pants
paddles the pages of a flipchart.
Headings fly by like weather. Meanwhile
the slob in the borrowed shirt (Creative
Writing and Film Studies) inwardly weeps,
shambling, manic and ursine down tunnels
of yesterday's whisky. Through booze ruined
memory he flees from the here and now
- the smoke reek on his clothes and breath
the stale stink of death in his pores - chasing
shadows and ghosts - his father, his marriage,
the amused indifference of his children
- hunted in turn by his own scary monster -
a rotting zombie, a dead man still walking,
the mutilated carcass of his self respect.

What should we do when confronted
by depression, either our own or someone else's
when that someone is entrusted to our care?
asks the woman in the floral pants.
Apparently there is no right or wrong.
No final answer exists. So just take care.

The slob in the borrowed shirt,
too tight, loaned him by a friend when
he woke at first light on his lounge floor
after a couple of hours of uneasy sleep,
tries to stay awake. He blinks and stares
still unaware and really too far gone to care
about the storm approaching his shanty town.

She drives a car with personalised plates
and tows behind her, like motherless lambs
shivering in the straw of a trailer,

9

or a kid, hidden under a sideboard,
her own anger and fear, her own lack of limits.
Apparently, in the interest of widening participation,
colleges are admitting the beautiful but insane
and she, in the interests of nothing save
her brave, bewildered, sad and greedy heart,
will make him need art and make him feel pain,
as she brings him back to life again.

typewritten poem to my bank manager

Dear Sir,
        These hammered keys to love,
these unlocked streams of thought unshaped by sense,
these insatiable demands for money I do not have,
the desperate and finite nature of my fruitless excuses
for losing it, for blowing it, for not having
a tight enough rein or a cool enough grip;
somewhere between these ragged parameters
(or do I mean perimeters and do you even care?)
the life slowly leaks from this living I eke.

And so, Dear Mr, Mrs, Ms, or Sir, I refer
you to your letter of the 5th inst. in which
you, in turn, refer to a missive of mine
that went missing some months since,
when the moon was, as you might remember
if your memory serves you well, hid in what Milton
once called its "vacant interlunar cave"
and I, perhaps, in fact more likely than perhaps,
was drunk, and faxed the fucking thing to Venus
rather than your high street branch, but anyway, in which,
in reply to your earlier requests for the money
you have been charging me for lending me money
and for writing letters to tell me what we both already know,
that all the aforementioned moneys are still owed,
I quoted some lines written by one H.Ledbetter,
not the freemason who has the plumbers' shop,
the business plan and the brother on the council,
but the other one,
Leadbelly, the guitarist, singer, songwriter and poet,
first name Huddie, a muddy skinned man who did time
for another's death and who wrote, and I quote,
as I did in the letter you apparently never received:
"If life was a thing that money could buy
The rich would live and the poor would die."

11

Tell me. What's your take on Leadbelly's riff?
Is there hope encoded in that "if"?
Or are you and I agreed that greed, or what Conrad
once called "a pitiless and rapacious folly"
will see us all shot to hell in a bucket?

Has the bank taken a position on this option? Is it exposed?
They are, after all, these tales of murder got away with
and murder punished, our culture. As surely as Shakespeare,
shylocks, loansharks, dreadlocks or the needles still scouring
old blues and new fortunes from the hissing Bakelite grooves
of race records. Whose voices and songs tell our shared tale?
Whose bent backs and shot brains bore the cost of its telling?

Shooting blind craps in a glittering gangster built city
infested with news crews and cameras; - this too plays a part in
making art, I think. How about you? Do you ever, like Blake,
wonder if in ancient time those feet walked here,
or what dread hand made all t'ings;
banks rich, me skint, English pastures,
Asian tigers, holy lamb and royal fucking mint.

Should we open, alongside my account, a conversation?
Or is your letter the last before my debt's written off
and sold, at discount, to other more free-form organisations
further down the food chain where life is more brutish
and brief and the key to success blind fear?
How does it feel, incidentally, to be on your own?

Look, I could sit and chew the fat for hours with you
over these half remembered fragments of this thing that,
because it is shared, we call our culture, but the money,
I am afraid - since it seems my letters, unlike yours,
are worth, in this world, nothing - I still do not have.

Yours etc.

The Ghost of Tom Joad

a zoo during recession

In a cage between the sea lions
and the monkey house, a starling shakes
rain from its feathers and swoops from a perch
worn smooth by a troop of captured lemurs
and hauls a wriggling gift from the English earth.

The lemurs are invisible now - gone
Wherever lemurs go when they pop their clogs.
They say that, sensing what was waiting
Up the pipe for them, half went mad.
But this is only speculation.

They were victims of a catastrophe
- a storm of shifting points
and tumbling stock that left them
powerless as it circled the earth.

Below the dead unbending branches,
through which the lemurs hurled themselves,
grass grows again. The natural world
(there is no other) always works.
It dictates what we see. Our gaze
is conditional. These bars divide us
from what is indivisible.

for martin hiatt

This poem
handwritten but printed
in American Typewriter
- there are nowadays names
and words for almost everything -
is about Martin, who until he died in a fire
would come to the Source where we'd read and talk
and pick up the mic and wing it.

He'd tell true stories
that some nights would take flight
and some nights fall apart

- that's how things go with an improvised art -

and once, with interior weather just so
and the planets all aligned just right
he told us that hitchhiking all alone,
escaping nothing headed nowhere,
in a field somewhere near Dumfries
he saw a unicorn and it troubled him
because he knew unicorns don't exist
and yet he could see it.

It was white, with beads of rainwater
in its mane and it leaned over a barbed
wire fence in the moonlight
and just now, if you were listening
and/or reading this - you saw it too

and it was as real as the Great Wall of China
Or the taste of a tangerine or tomorrow
Or a flicker of flame you imagine
As you slowly fall asleep.

poem for james

He'd come from The Griffin, was on his way to the Club,
when he walked through a door in the world.
He didn't know why, only that he wanted to.

He remembered when he was young.
He used to swim in the River Petteril
near the Old Railway Club and swing out
over the water on a rope tied to a tree branch.
There was no money about and he wore
second hand clothes. He remembered bike rides
to the country on his big brother's bike
picking blackberries and scrumping apples.
His mum put food on the table for him
and for two brothers and a sister.

Some things you can remember others you can't.
Some you don't want to, but you do.

His mum, was like any mum, he said,
- loving, caring, protecting her brood.
A hundred percent for the kids.
But now, with his sister and his dad dead,
and two years of marriage, twenty seven
years of courting, some drinking, some fighting,
some robbing, some prison all behind him
- (a roundabout - still spinning - from which
he says he's stepped off) he watches as hour by hour,
day by day, an illness, takes his mum
and who she was further and further away
from him and he knows he was always frightened;
- of people, of crowds, of language and of life.

But now rage has turned to acceptance he knows
sadness and self knowledge are all that will endure;
- that everything else - love, family, friendship
and the dreams and memories of these things -

will one day just be blown like dust or straw
from the scrubbed stone step at the kitchen door.

where eden flows

on the stretched skin of now

the song
                    (bloody footprints in snow)

& dance
                    (skinned knuckles on ice)

drum us forward
                    & back

longing
                    (weight of breath in air)

to say what we know
no one can say

& know what they say
no one can know

                    (weight of ink on a page)

& see the slow
                    (ghost of a chance)

impossible miracle

& Eden

flow

lines written on the floods in the west of the county

Before I built a wall I'd ask to know
What I was walling in or walling out,
And to whom I was like to give offense.

Robert Frost

The waters weigh heavy, the rains come down
but fall heavier on our neighbours' town
until a bridge or a bank gives way
and a human life is swept away
in a torrent from which a hand,
like a snapped fencepost, reaches up
and seeks tight hold of another's hand
and grasps instead only darkness and rain,
a story repeated again and again
as someone's father, someone's son
is suddenly and irrevocably gone
lost to this storm and the storms to come.

But all I really want to say
is none of this will go away.
Who tells the truth? Who's a liar?
Must we build the floodwalls higher?

Our neighbour, and our neighbour's house,
is just an empathetic heartbeat
or two clicks of a mouse from being us
and on the wilder shores of a shared sea
some say that him and her and you and me
are anyway all one and though we can pick
from the mud's cold stink what we think
was built to last, and construct a future
from a broken past, somewhere a father
somewhere a daughter, will again lie lost
beneath brown fields of water and green hills
that rise and fall and rise again like the waves
that lap the cold faces of the stones.

18

None of this will go away.
This hard place is where we must stay.
Who tells the truth? Who's a liar?
Must we build the fallen walls still higher?

A family, one family, are branches
of a single tree bent by flood waters
until it tears and breaks and because
where once there was land there is no land
and where once there was water the water
is gone, those that remain to carry on
the building, rebuilding and compromise,
the daily humdrum of the quid pro quo,
are made hostage to ever more savage
changes of season and the slow slack reach
of the tide within us that follows
the implacable transit of this cold moon.

Land and water, earth and sky
are contiguous, neighbours endlessly
negotiating ownership of a shared space
while the boundary lines on maps that define
the limits of nations and neighbourliness
are marked in this world by razor wire,
a stand tap, a shelter, shared scraps and a fire.
And on some distant desert track,
driven not by water but by its lack,
a family - like a river in spate -
seeks to find the only place it can go
but is held back by the barrel of a gun.
This time will come. Has already begun.

Who tells the truth? And who's a liar?
Must we build the walls around us higher?
Grieve, if you can, for what's lost.
Taste, if you can, a new day.

None of this will go away.

the ways of the hand - after martin heidegger

The hand reaches and extends,
receives and welcomes
- and not just things:
the hand extends itself
and receives its own welcome
in the hands of others.

The hand holds.
The hand carries.
The hand designs and signs,
presumably because man is a sign…

the hand's gestures run
everywhere through language,
in their most perfect purity precisely
when man speaks by being silent.

And only when man speaks
does he think - not the other way round
as metaphysics still believes.

Every motion of the hand
in every one of its works
carries itself through thought
and every bearing of the hand
bears itself in that element.

sleight of hand

Morning is a child's kite flown across the sky
its precarious, tethered, wind balanced
flight just another juggler's stunt.
But while an eye follows an orange, a button, a burnished coin
- the sun's slow changes through its loop -
the quickened blood sent racing by these tricks
involves itself in a daily commerce
- hands, feet and heart,
human aims that deny our separateness
or make of it a quirky art.

Evening, a stranger in a familiar hat,
silently tips it to our transactions
and from beneath spill stars and lighted signs
as behind a drawn curtain and a doorbell
(that as a kid I'd ring then run)
each day seeks resolution in rest, in running
repairs and rehearsals for tomorrow
until, finally, each alone in sleep's far reaches
we are held tight as a handful of pebbles.

Moonlight through a window reveals a sleeper
and at the foot of his bed a torn, patched kite
while scattered silent as stars round his head
are buttons, coins, oranges, a hat.

A pebble on the windowpane wakes him.

the drunken waterlilies

The waterlilies by the mill
Are drunk today on gin
While the wind blows casual whispers
Through their earth-tied flowering sin.

The rotten bloom is open
The frightened bloom is closed
The shoots and leaves and fractured buds
Are scattered round the roads.

The papermill turns slowly
To make a snow white paper soul,
The waterlilies chuckle drunk
Down by the waterhole.

Tides

first meeting

Slowly approaching the shore,
I watched a man skim stones out over a lake,
Sure that however long he browsed the beach
For the right pebble, however much spin
His wrists and fingers might give each skipped step
Through air, over water, his uneven
Sporting contest with time and gravity
Could have only one outcome.

For over a surface as dark as an x-ray
A smeared shadow kept pace with each stone;
Waiting to claim it. They touched, parted,
Touched again, each momentary join and separation
Rippling the mirror to a dance of light
Until, momentum spent, stone and insubstantial twin
Were fused in a final skittering interface
And sank from sight.

Below, a char's belly scraped a lakebed
Littered with ancient debris; - and time
Flowed slow as a glacier.

Above, eyes looked down at the water's edge to see,
Pierced by sunlight, shocked by recognition,
The image of a man reflected back,
Emptyhanded, arm outstretched, pebble gone.

Whose were the eyes? Whose the face staring back?
Were both mine? As the man turned away
His flawed ghost flickered, fractured, became
Air and water, light and darkness, the space
Between fingertips, nothing. I watched and waited
In the slow, cold current.

low tide

They walk through the grey morning,
eyes blinking, minds tired,
minds blinking but eyes still seeing
the estuarine scum crazed with birds' footprints,
and they talk, talk, talk, talk, talk their amphetamine babble
as the slicked mud sucks each step at their shoes.

> Say, don't ya remember, man?
> Remember. Remember? Remember what?
> The dog days, man. Yeah, the cold rat days.
> The days we thought death was ugly.
> Just water on a stone, water on a stone.
> Ya remember the guy with the tattoo? Some
> woman's stupid name on his arm? Yamean
> the guy from the bar? The one who we...
> Yeah, that's the guy. Crazy as a piece of string.
> Mad as a meat axe and askin' for it.
> What'd he do? Yamean ya don't remember? Nah.
> I askya, man, ain't there no balance left to
> strike no more.

Voices in a bar at lunchtime
and sunlight through the windows.
Old orders fading, new ones only fragments,
last ones yet to be called.
Shapes in smoke, dominoes, darts and faces
surround them as they scrape caked dirt from their shoes
while, outside, sea swallows river,
erasing each cut in the clay,
each mark in the mud.

the disappearance of captain jack

Hungover with my brother in law
I wandered the flat estuary sands
to the point at which the River Ribble
breaches its channel & disintegrates
into the sea's distant, endless murmur.

Both tired from chasing the outgoing tide
& scattered families & tribes of kids
& weary from alcohol abuse & walking,
we stopped to dry out (just our shoes) and rest
on a bleak bare salt stripped tree trunk
born down from the fells of Westmorland
moons before this Moon of the Drying Grass

    & there
                        look
       suddenly
                              where he points
                       on the flat scummy strand
dead as driftwood
             tugged torn & surrendered by the sea

                            a beached yacht

  & behind the salt smeared port
       in the cabin's dank varnished womb
  caught unborn between a rock & a hard place
with head in hands & eyes glued on the empty
    bottle & glass before him could be a man

- quite possibly Captain Jack, a.k.a.
Kintpuash, Having the Water Brash,
who lived and died one hundred years ago,
a Modoc chief too brave, straight & honest
for his own good who believed life was sweet
& ended up hung for shooting a general

& exhumed & embalmed by grave robbers
who toured the gaslit eastern seaboard cities
& displayed dead Kintpuash at carnivals
ten cents a pop (all true, all true, all true)
until one night he escaped
& became Captain Jack, time mariner
& traveller on the wind & tides
or, since the dead so seldom escape
their condition, quite possibly not.

For when we wiped the caked crystal
from the porthole & peered inside
there was no one.   No Captain Jack.
No bottle. No rock. Only this hard place.

Time & tide have wiped the yacht from the shore,
the salt crystal from our fingers, the dirty glass
from beneath our palms. Our reflections in
the still dark surface of oblivion's well
are as fleeting as a taste on our lips,
a smile in our eyes, a thought in your head...
but with no vessel to contain his voice,
no mouth, no captain's chest, no tongue to tease
or sculpt his thoughts, Captain Jack has vanished,
an invisible bird in the sky's blue eaves
from whose unruly nest of words once flew these:

"Let everything be wiped out, washed out,
and let there be no more blood."

Rested and dry, my brother and I
- twin mickeymice thus far still unscathed -
left the broken tree behind and, chasing
families and dreams of lost fathers and sons,
through tumbling anvils of cloud wandered on.

dancing horse

The white man knows how to make everything
but he does not know how to distribute it.
                              Sitting Bull to Annie Oakley, 1885

In 1885, when Tatanka Iyotake left Bill Cody's
triumphant heap big wild west spectacle
his old boss gave him a white sombrero
& an old show horse trained to do tricks
at the sound of gunshots. Accepting
these gifts with cool imperious pride, Sitting Bull
returned to Standing Rock, resistance
& the slow murder of his nation.

Four years later - count how many moons & suns -
word came from Wovoka, Paiute mystic,
that by a lake, beyond the Shining Mountains
in Nevada, Jesus had come to earth.

Many hundreds - thousands - journeyed to greet him
& saw the scars on his hands & cheeks.
Moccasins covered his feet. "Dance," he told them.
"Dance the Ghost Dance and you shall be raised up.
Your ancestors shall also be raised and a wave
shall pass across the earth & afterwards
you & the dead who went before you
shall inherit new soil, running water
sweet grass & all that was taken from you."

Since pilgrims by nature are believers
they danced until they knew each step
sure & certain as their own names
& Jesus Christ it is said flew to
& fro above their heads
& taught them songs

                    & word & music & dance
spread like wildfire moonshine firewater
foolishness among their poor, tired & hungry
reservations. They danced to bring back ghosts

& the powers that be, like they always are,
- scared of what they don't get -
did what they always do. They started making arrests.

When the Indian police called at his tepee
Sitting Bull of the Hunkpapa Teton Sioux
pulled on his pants & called for his horse.
A crowd grew angry, tempers flared
& Red Tomahawk shot Sitting Bull dead;
- palla in la testa - a bullet in his head
while his horse, spurred on by the sound,
stood, turned, raised a hoof and stamped on the ground
then bowed in the frozen, bloodstained snow.

The seasons blow down the years to today
- count again the suns, count the moons -
and Nevada, now ceded to the military and the mob,
is one more argent circle of hell where
stealth weapons carve whispers in the air
and radiation gibbers in the bomb-tainted earth
and rivers and desert aquifers fill gamblers'
fountains and flaming waterfalls, and all
flows away faster than it can be fed
- and of reincarnated Messiah
no more is said.

dreams of emigration

He travelled round the world
courtesy of Qantas and money
left by his dear dead dad
and as the earth that for two
telescoped days and nights had unfurled
beneath his flight continued to turn and turn
and turn in its slow endless circle
and the sun blazed and burned
to the heart of another day
in God's own country he walked,
jetlagged and breached, into the booming
surf on a Queensland beach
and let the breakers bash
his body and the Pacific
stream through his fingers
and watched the silver flicker of a shoal
of fish suspended in the translucent
curling eave of a tumbling wave
while he dreamed whodunits.

The uniform coil of the rifled
barrel that sends the bullet spinning
and the spiral spear of the narwhal's
unicorn spike: what forces form
and drive these disparate things?
What binds them together/tears them apart?
From what fissured space do we cleave
the cracked imperfect grammar of the heart?
From what loss has love been made
and what roots forever severed
by the bight of falling spade?

The waves smashed through his memory's
gape and gash and the sand
flayed the skin from his face
until he was almost gone,

31

first next to nothing
then no one,
just another buried voice
in the sweet, ghostwritten mystery
of light.

aussie hospitality

Around the barbie
or on the beach they say
or seem to say:

"The sun is ours,
the warm air is ours.
Let us share with you
those things you don't have."

The sound of cicadas
saws seamless time into segments.
We tilt cold brown bottles
to suncracked lips and toast
God's own country.

But all this talk of paradise
is whistling in the dark.
This place is not hospitable,
there is harshness at its empty heart.

The aborigines, whose heart it is,
know how to traverse
this sacred space.

But they stare into darker fire,
and sip at stronger spirits
as belief leaks like tar
from their fractured dreamtime.

neighbours

One blazing Queensland morning,
knowing I was English, Mr Kazantzakis
called me across his lush green lawn,
flattened, seeded, sprinkled, weeded,
to see his Triumph, a '68 Dolomite,
and trade clichés, - "She's a beaut.
They don't make them like this anymore," -
and on the car's lovingly burnished bonnet,
in a bungalow in suburbia, in a garage
hot, oppressive, and constricting as a coffin,
while my family waited next door,
he led me slowly through his boxes of snaps.

There were pictures of fathers, grandfathers,
a first wife dead, a second wife gone,
- "Shot through on me, she did, on her eighty-second birthday,"
great-grandfathers and their brothers solemn
in the skirts and waistcoats of the old country.
There were family groups and friends
at weddings and weddings and, later, christenings,
anniversaries, holidays and union outings
and, in black and white, posed on a beach front,
arms folded forever over his bodybuilder's chest,
a son, drowned in the mouth of the Yarra.

And every few pages,
amongst workmates and family,
were photos of fish.

Hundreds and hundreds of them.

"That was a Tuesday. Bob phoned and told me
the mackerel were running.
That was a Wednesday.
That was October last year.
A Monday, I think."

all alike, all laid out in lines
across bright sunlit slabs of metal and stone,
deep blocks of shadow, blue water backgrounds,
and in each dead scale this geometry
of divided light was fragmented
into tiny rainbows.

Perhaps he sought something
left behind and lost, or revenge
on a sea he thought had crossed him.
Or maybe he saw the fish as a pause for breath
in a dense, unruly, endless, streaming song,
or a punctuation that made sense of dreams
and the promises of a new country
he would one day call home.

morning in andalucía

A daddy longlegs' dangling legs,
thin as a scratch on glass,
write shadows on the wall
of a whitewashed church.

Above a ravine, on limestone crags
bleached whiter than bone or churchwall,
cacti cling in spiky, tuberous clumps,
fleshy old men staring into rootless eternity.

A goat's bell hammers flat a melody
and a buzzard's taut, tattered wing
sculpts invisible blue shapes
of columns of shimmering air
where each breath lifts a weight
from what is possible.

the bus driver

The bus driver gave his passengers
A brilliant, speed crackled commentary
as he hammered his city bus along
the smallest roads in the world,
Keeping up constant comic/philosophic banter
As he bore down on a tight corner where a tattooed tourist
Carried a case of beercans on his head.

Toot, hiss, airbrakes, doors, ding,
Dolphins, lions, Merry Christmas,
Want a cigarette, ding, got any blues?
I will them to you. It was limited,
Repetitive. Relatively speaking,
The island was tiny, a tiny world
But he could do it, this work, he
Could be, he could weave this silver shuttle
Through the island's tapestry of voices
Like wind through the strings of a lyre
In high, far off Aeolian hills. Three islands
North of here, St John had sat shaking in a cave
As the promises of Revelation unfolded
In the darkness. God's light illuminating
The moist darkness. Four islands south
Of here, the last century's depopulation is reversed.
The island's diaspora return with dollars for the economy
and New Jersey plates to decorate the walls
Of tumbledown family homes. And here
On this island, over this earth, Roman, Greek,
And Turk have fought. Germans, Italians
And British battled to bloody standstills
In its dirt. And now ten years of tourism have done
What four thousand decades could not. This place,
His home, is changed forever. And ever. Ding.

Dolphins, lions, doctors, kings, oops, no brakes,
No really, only kidding. We're safe here.

dangerous crossroads

Down at the crossroads
where Robert Johnson made his lonely deal,
there's now a hundred million souls
with a billion ways to feel.
On the paths that lead away from us
and the paths that brought us here,
there's a hundred thousand voices
all fighting for our ear;
people yelling, people selling,
people buying, people dying,
people dealing, people stealing,
freak shows, breakdowns, peek shows, shakedowns,
gamblers, grumblers, ramblers, stumblers.
There's lovers, children, husbands, wives,
who work and wonder, who watch their lives
and dreams like ragged flags unfurled
at each dangerous crossroads of our world.
So here we are at (fill in blank)
the transglobal, multicultural knees-up Saturday night
where we celebrate cultural diversity and fight
against human perversity. But time's heartbeat moves on.
We're here then we're gone. But the drum
and the heartbeat we dance to beats on;
it beats out a rhythm, a pattern, a mystery,
we sway to its song in the dancehalls of history…

He was the Memphis Miracle, a hillbilly flash,
a truck-driving dandy, son of poor white trash,
hanging out on the corner, combing his hair,
sifting different rhythms that were floating in the air.
All shook up - together - country music & the blues
with some money in his pocket he sang blue suede shoes.
He rattled teenage cages with his jailhouse rock
but grew greasy rich and middle-aged singing Vegas schlock.
Was this truly the King? Does anybody know?
Or just a fat dead guy in a sequinned baby-grow?

Whatever your answer, remember, back there for a little while,
Elvis rocked the world with his style.

Music is a journey, from note to note,
migration is a journey, boat after boat,
a story's just a journey to the end,
friendship's just a journey,
you take it with your friends.
So don't fear it when you hear it, let it in,
its fingers that are rapping on the skin of a drum.
So let it come into your heart;
feel your feelings dance together
then feel them dance apart.

Let's go back in time to the Mississippi Delta,
where every black woman who was born there felt a pain
and every black man who was born there felt the same;
sing a song, far from home, and the blues becomes its name…

But the years fly by the crossroads all the time,
the future's like a freight train on the line.
Now the blues is full of laughter, played loose and sweet,
with an improvised melody that dances round the beat;
it's a new church music in the street,
but that's not all,
it's the music of the juke joint and Carnegie Hall,
but when the hall is empty and the crowd has gone
and at the hotel door stands a man with a horn,
now the horn's in its case the colour of his face,
means - suddenly - there ain't no room in the place…
It's the same old story in every bourgeois town;
you can live for the music but the life can wear you down,
but there's hope in every note when push comes to shove
that all those dumb and ugly feelings can be conquered by love,
and that's the cool beauty of jazz,
the red hot magic of jazz,
it's real….
it's how we feel….
it's just…………………jazz.

Music is a journey, from note to note,
migration is a journey, boxcars and riverboats,
a story's just a journey to the end,
friendship's just a journey,
you take it with your friends.
So don't fear it when you hear it, let it in,
its fingers that are rapping on the skin of a drum.
So let it come into your heart;
feel your feelings dance together
then feel them dance apart.

Don't want to get romantic, frantic, pedantic or semantic
so let's take a trip back across the Atlantic
to Europe, the old world, the bought and sold world, the solid
gold world,
that made the grade, through its trade.
So what have you got? They'll trade the lot.
They'll trade a coin for a candle for a can
and a can for some blankets for a man
and a man for a coin for a gun,
just hear the gypsy fiddle play on...

She's got holes in her shoes - the poor European blues -
just hear the gypsy fiddle play on

He's got nowhere to sleep so he's sleeping in the street,
just hear the gypsy fiddle play on

See them down on their luck, see them shoved in cattle trucks,
and hear the gypsy fiddle play on

See them huddle under cover, hear the bombers flying over,
and hear the gypsy fiddle play on

It's playing out the memory in the blood
of a cousin, of a lover, of a mother in the mud.
It plays a song for a man with a gun,
it plays a song for a man with a drum,
it plays a song for the soldiers when they come...

Music is a journey, from note to note,
migration is a journey, with no passport and no coat,
a story's just a journey to the end,
friendship's just a journey,
you take it with your friends.
So don't fear it when you hear it, let it in,
its fingers that are rapping on the skin of a drum.
So let it come into your heart;
feel your feelings dance together
then feel them dance apart.

There's a High Wind in Jamaica, you can hear it blow.
Cockerel's getting restless, you can hear him crow.
Hurricane's coming, the storm clouds grow
then...CRACK...just listen to the thunder and lightning,
rain rattles on the roof all night it's frightening...

Daybreak comes and the storm's blown out
but look at the wreckage that's been scattered all about;
cane's as flat as a hat that a mule stepped on
and that means the work and the money's all gone
but…"Hey, take a look at this in The Gleaner
we could maybe go to Inglan get a job as a cleaner
or a cook or a guard or a driver or a nurse
cheer up now, baby, tings could be plenty worse..."

Six months later, leaning on the rail of ship
as families on the dockside wave them off on their trip
into history. They're on a great migration,
an invitation from a nation to a nation
to help rebuild a country that the war's torn down,
working in the factories, in the cities, in the towns...

And the years fly by, in the blink of an eye,
we're all working here together under England's rainy skies,
working here together though the work sometimes runs dry
and our children and grandchildren - into jungle and dub -
are dancing here together in a multicultural club.

Because music is a journey, from note to note,
migration is a journey, boat after boat,
a story's just a journey to the end,
friendship's just a journey,
you take it with your friends.
So don't fear it when you hear it, let it in,
its fingers that are rapping on the skin of a drum.
So let it come into your heart;
feel your feelings dance together
then feel them dance apart.

The past's a place that we can't go,
but the past is all we know.
Our dreams might not be all that clear
but, our dreams, they brought us here.
And music is a journey and a home.

poem for flute and didgeridoo

it begins with nothing
save the heart's first startled push

and we
start with nothing
save this vibration of empty air
recalling wind and thunder and the creak
of trees in a heat haze, the dissolving shore,
the blurring of waves into one wave
the sound of water in a stream bed
threading our invisible dreaming
through this indivisible world

where in Bamako a moth batters at a light
and a gecko still waits for the start of the rain
on the gigantic mud walls of a village mosque

this world where in Naples or Bucharest or just round the
corner from here a junkie nods off in an empty room

this world where lovers leave no trace of their passage
in the grass but see migrating birds
echoed in the shape of a shell

this world where beneath southern stars
a jukebox in a desert bar falls silent

and the spirits of animals, the mothers of mountains
the fathers of forest and the children of clouds
and birds swim through the vibrating
sinew of the moment

to this moment, this here and now,
that began, as it always begins
in nothing

the mad accordion

Take the box,
shake the box,
if you must
(and you must)
snap the hasp
and break the locks
and take out the mad accordion...

Let your fingers stroke its keys
let its slinky plaintive wheeze
lead you through the darkening trees
to a landing stage upon a lake shore
where reeds creak and dandelion spore
and duck down dance down to the water
where, beneath the silver surface, spiky perch fins glisten
and now - between heartbeats - you pause, and you listen...

This time, hold it close, soon it will be gone
like the secret dreams locked in the heart
of the mad accordion...

So amongst the shadows of the builders'
breezeblock open your shoulders, raise your head,
play the mad squeezebox until you're dead,
until every prodigal daughter, every runaway son
walks home across the windblown water
on a winding stair of thought. Trade each note
for the next note, there are only these, there are no more
and each note that's gone leaves nothing behind,
no stepping stones lead back to the shore.
Squeeze the mad squeezebox, squeeze diamonds to dust
or stretch air into insubstantial chains of melody,
a living entity that still, through stillness, leads you on...

Find yourself a key,
play it, play it,
(as if you were free)
play it, play it,
play it till time bends,
play it, play it,
play it till you lose friends
play it play it
play it till the song ends
play it play it
all alone
play it weary to the bone
play it, play it
play it till your fingers are sore
play it, play it...

Now take a deep breath
and play it some more.

Silver fish, like lightning
play the mad accordion

Nightjars in the shadows
play the mad accordion

The momentum in the breaking waves
plays the mad accordion

The patients in their hospital beds
walk through the trapdoors in their heads
to play the mad accordion

Bugs bunny with his looney tunes
on a million tvs on a million afternoons
still plays the mad accordion

stretch a cage around the sun
with the words of the mad accordion

Play me, play me till I break
or the world is broken and I belong,
play me till each word is spoken
and each spoken word becomes a song

So says

(or maybe prays)

the man who plays the man

who played the man who is played

by

the mad accordion

Islands

island perspectives

The creative act is not performed by the artist alone; the spectator brings the work in contact with the external world by deciphering and interpreting its inner qualifications and thus adds his contribution to the creative act.

Marcel Duchamp

And then they said, "Yeah, we gonna put him so far back in jail this time, 'till they gonna have to pump air into him."

Bo Diddley, "Cops & Robbers"

1. misdirection

I think it was after the takeover
but before the troops arrived
- anyway, it was after his mother died -
that his behaviour started to become unpredictable.
Eventually he stopped answering the letters they sent him
and they decided - rightly I think - that this was unacceptable.
So they asked me, because we had history, unfinished business,
to keep an eye on him. Which I did. Same as when we were
kids...

...because stone beats scissors
scissors beat paper
and paper beats stone.

My part in this was simple. All I had to do
was get him to open his mail again.
And on this particular morning, when he did,
tearing loose the lip of a jiffy with the half of the scissors
that his lover left behind when - (this too
I had helped arrange) - her posting to the city
in the south came through, he found,
wrapped in tissue, cushioned in a cuckoo spit
of plastic bubbles, a stone. That's all.

But the beautiful part was this: the person
who sent it, a tattooed woman with a white apple,
thought the man she was sending it to was someone else.
Took me a while to get my head round that but eventually
I was okay with it. You see, you might want them to,
but people don't change. It's always the same:

stone breaks scissors
scissors cut paper
and paper wraps stone.

Later that morning - (picture it) -
while walking on the shore of our inland sea
he was persuaded - (they're good at this kind of thing) -
to trade the pebble for a ferry ticket
- one way only - printed on paper as grey
and recycled as the sky. It cost roundabout
a ton, and I sometimes wonder if, later,
when the mist came down,
headed for a destination that
- to his credit - he took on trust,
high in grey space between unseen places,
dreaming along to the diesel turbines
that shook the ship's rail he remembered
the promise, silent as the sleeping earth,
that the woman with the white apple
had made to someone else:

that stones would float
and paper blunt scissors
and scissors cut stone.

It doesn't do to think too hard about motives
for what does and doesn't get done.
The same rules apply to almost everyone.
Even so, I like to think that, for once,
- because (unofficially speaking) on the island
where the ferry docked they're off the radar
and on a different clock - they decided not to meet

him on the quay where the harbour seals
grow fat and dirty round the fetid drains,
that, instead, they let him wander into peaceful
internal exile - and that amongst the dog roses
that choke the lanes beneath the mountain
he traded what little his journey had left him
for one last stone and a list of names
and that they let him walk, backward and forward,
through a maze of games and days to this one...

today: in a city in the south
a woman deletes a padlocked memo
and powers down a white apple while
a boy with a bike with a broken chain
- (and yes, I confess, that was once me) -
sits trying to figure out how to get home.
And here comes our man, his friend, trying his best
to second guess fate with nothing to his name
save a cheerful spirit and a fistful of rain.

Sometimes he's there, sometimes he's only half there,
and sometimes, he's gone. And I can live with that...
because stone will break scissors
scissors cut paper and paper wrap stone

but time and tide will break stone into sand
as long as the sea washes over the land.

2. what is this room through which we walk?

What is this room through which we pass
but the senses' momentary persistence
in memory? What are its walls but dreams?
Is the soul solid, defined
by a single act - an iron spike jammed
into the husks and broken glass
on a dirt beach at the city's edge -
or is it as ramshackle and makeshift

as the shanties tumbling across the
gullies and steep hills and that rise behind
the torn billboards and empty banks
of our failed republic? Or has it less body
than a leaf, or the breeze that says:
Unless we die we cannot be born?

I have sleepwalked through this house,
fingers pressed to the bulging weary walls
of my eyes, nudging open doors and windows
with a shrugged shoulder and a smile,
seeking passage through a crack of light
to a place where the air no longer echoes
with the simplistic rhythms of the news,
where the feral fairground screams of children
who want something
or want something to stop
have been replaced by silence,
and on a cracked and grimy pane,
amongst the first collisions of dust and rain,
I have found, written in a stranger's hand:
Unless I have been born I cannot die.

No safety lies in this ruin. It is not backdrop
or endpoint to an ancient process. Instead,
unacknowledged, ever present, it has been waiting
for us to catch up and catch on
- the trap in every earnest airless stanza,
the breath in every lightless cell,
and only the slapdash magic with which,
to spite it, we continue to connect
one damned thing to another will save us
from the simple message of the storm:
Because we is dead I am born.

3. cage wrestling for dummies

They say that, at the far end of the island
beyond the old settlement and the half
buried white stones of the Celtic maze
in the warren of rusting containers
left high and dry by the slump in trade
is a mirror which can do a kind of magic

but that to find it, first you must
look amongst all the other stuff that
local superstition insists is in there too:
- the old star charts and the maps
that since they closed the borders have been withdrawn,
the obsolete textbooks that, now geography
has been redefined, are no longer needed,
the cult paperbacks and ticket stubs,
the tinfoil and popped plastic bubbles
that held the pills that got you so confused,
the receipts for stuff that you refused to remember,
the worthless, stone roughened blue green jewels
of bottle glass scavenged from the beaches where
each day, on the high tide, we still watch
the ferry's arrival or departure…
the old names of the cities: - all these things
are here, they say, within a cage of rain.

There are even some who to this day believe
you can find in love's indifferent ebb and flow
anything at all, lost however long ago,
that round a corner you may come across
a dog, or a man, barking at a breaking wave
or - if you get far enough into it - bits of stories,
broken down in pieces and stored side by side:
- random as an unborn child, falling blossom,
bricks in a wall, a row of boxes left unticked,
all that - to save our lives - we left behind.

Because we have had to learn new skills

53

- like how to read between the lines
of those papers that have escaped embargo -
I know that should I need to go and look
amongst these things that I'll find you there
- by a fire, in a book, a hand printed letter
or the kern, curl and shank of a line of type,
a skeleton dance of signs encoding
thoughts and gestures better captured in light.

So look around. Don't hold back…
Did I say you'd find a mirror there?
You'll find it here too. Let me show you
its meagre magic. The door opens out, not in.
Step outward through it and into the world.

4. word from the island

First they sent me a card that said

a parachute from yesterday
is already falling towards you

and later - in spring - just before the parades -
in a brown A4 envelope an old school photograph
with all the faces blacked out save two - me and you -

and then, after a bright and tranquil summer
your picture book arrived in which all the names
that once attached to all those scratched out faces

- Abira, Aban, Ali, Eddie, Farrah, Gabir, Hassan -

you'd now given as titles - as if they were beautiful
intricate artworks - to the sea dumped heaps
of ropes, bones and bottles that litter the island beaches

or to objects left behind
in the empty doorways of abandoned shanties,

or found trapped in the bulldozed rubble of government slums
or hung from a telephone pole in the shank of a broken road

each logged and dated image becoming
- in the absence of anything else to which a name might fix -
the matter and tactile substance of memory itself.

Ibrahim - *merciful and kind* -
a rust coloured glove in a fisherman's net
Rosedana - *angel protector* - the bars to a baby's cot
Shabeen - *loyal follower* - a single shoe on a doorstep
Sanaa - *brilliance* - scrawled on a wall behind an oil drum.

I'll give you this much: -
maybe you've nothing better to do with your time
but from next to nothing
save stubborn desolate disordered whim
you have managed to make a memorial to qualities not strong

or tough enough to survive
these mainland times of ambient fear
where anything can be made or made to disappear.
But so what? You're there. I'm here. And I have done

what I think you would expect me to do
and scratched out the last faces. First me. Then you.
Or was it you? Then me? All gone. Like history.

footprints

Stepping out of my back door last Friday,
taking letters to the post, my kids to school,
I saw the bird's footmarks in the concrete
which the builders laid in the yard last year
were full of rain and I thought of Louie
whom I called auntie though in reality
she was my gran's cousin or something like that
and in whose back garden was a dead tree
on which my brother and I used to climb,
and who had a husband, Uncle Harry,
who'd been gassed in the trenches and who coughed
and who, I remember this quite clearly,
once watched TV with me and my brother,
(we were small, lying on a patchwork rug
in front of a fire, - hands on chins
staring up at the screen) and Jesse Owens
was running on a flickery old film,
black and white newsreel of the Berlin games
repeated now as history that we kids
were learning for the first shocking time,
and when Owens, the victor, offered his hand
and Hitler, the dictator, refused it,
Harry said softly, "He should've spat on him,"
and Louie told him to hush. And he did.

The ambiguity of all this scares me.
"Tell me, Uncle Harry," I want to ask,
though what difference it makes now he's dead
I don't know, - "Tell me who you meant.
Who did you think should have spat upon whom?"

These tracks left in my yard last year
by a bird I never saw made me think of Louie
because they made me think of a day
when my brother and I had sat and watched
Uncle Harry fixing a front gate hinge;

and he'd watched us watching him then
shifted his tools to show us the spot
on the step where years and years before,
two years before he'd ever been to war,
- before his path set hard the way paths do -
a passing cat had sunk a paw.

To us,
afterwards, that mark always seemed as full
of mystery as the lone footprint left
on the shore of Robinson Crusoe's island.

I see it still and recall how our thrilled
childish faces made Harry smile a rare smile
as his fingertips brushed absently
at the shadows of leaves that dappled
that single pawprint dimpled in cement.

Harry, Louie, Hitler, Jesse Owens,
my brother with whom when we grew older
I wrote kids' comics and stories to order,
gung ho stuff about good looking L.A.
fascists, sexy, easygoing action men
who loved children and hated paperwork
and whose talking cars, nuclear choppers
and smart weapons protected innocence
from the bad guys, often fanatic foreign terrorists
twisted by hatred and greed who planned
to blow the kids at the orphanage picnic sky high
with their crude bombs...all of it bullshit...
...all of these people are dead and gone now.

But sometimes still I meet their ghosts
in a memory mortgaged house whose doors
are unlocked by birds' footprints and cats' paws.

Nothing is set in stone.

lines written on an iou in corbridge

I lean on a wall in Corbridge,
pull up the drawbridge, disengage
and retreat into the sandy land of language

while he skates the curls and turns of an Arabic script
a dancing calligraphic fool standing still on a hill
the slow mo lean and fall of a stick stuck in snow.

So it goes.

We went skiing and seeing. Never missed a stitch.
Went to look. God knows, it was an open book.
We talked and turned pages. Talked, talked

talked till we were spent and the usual train
arrived and we were left to reinvent
our lives as if they counted.

drifter's escape

Just then a bolt of lightning,
shook the courthouse out of shape
and as everybody knelt to pray
the drifter did escape.

after Bob Dylan

1. flight

He blinked, shook what felt like sleep from his eyes
then seeking escape from a life gone shitty
he took the underground route from the city
along a canal constructed and worked
back when the bass sounds were fat and fashion
favoured jazzy belt buckles and boot straps
by which you could - if you could - pull yourself up,
or maybe it was two clicks of slippery history
back from there, back in the day
and the eroded shadows of a story
no one any longer really knows

and sluggish and powerful as a prayer
the stone scar in the hard earth compelled him
through the weed and bobbing plastic
beside the abandoned chemical plant,
across a still reach of smoking water
past the tag marks on the cement walls
and the bright, cantilevered new stadiums,
down the measured steps and liquid flights of locks
past sheep - shorn and fleeced - and the forlorn cheep
of a solitary cygnet, past a ruin full of feral screeches,
a gated estate and a manor house full of money

and in the cool, shadowed arch of a bridge
he heard a voice - perhaps from the ants
in the dusty cracks in the cobblestones

that in winter shine with frozen, slimy ice
or maybe it came from someplace within
the battered joke he had made of his heart -
and it whispered with a soft insistence
that would not be denied: "Come with me
past the silent drinkers in the Fool's Nook
through the swing bridge and the avenue of trees
to where what you want still waits to be discovered."

He watched the weather wizened walkers
with their maps and sunglasses, sticks and packs,
the narrow boats that rose on the water
through the numbered locks and bridges,
the milestones and measured, counted miles,
cities, mill towns, lockside stones worn smooth
by the repeated steps of generations
who had walked this clay lined cut and suddenly

he knew as surely as he knew his own name
that his flight was towards this family
of ghosts - men, women, kids, a dog, a cat,
some coins and a cooking pot - who
without ownership or significant fortune
had once, for a while, made the world work.

2. on the level

If you can get your head round
the idea that the you in this is really us
and that the us in this is the same as we but bigger
and the he in this poem is someone else but sometimes me
then maybe you'll see what he saw and he thought
as the boat carried him still further along
the channel built - for their daily bread -
by gangs of navvies now long dead.

You can't get off the track that's set for you.
Like the mapped out branches of a family tree
you can only go where the laid out streets

and arterial highways lead: letting you think you're free.

That (he thought) is the way that the world works.

Ambition, intrigue, love, suffering,
the incessant clamour of days
all demand response until
all that remains to break the cemetery's silence
is laughter - which was always more serious than tears.

Whether we're carpenters, bookbinders,
scriveners, lawyers, hauliers, tumescent adolescents,
dumb babes, senescent old men with sticks and stammers,
crones with boney fingers, expectant mamas,
drunks or vagrants or urchin children
speaking the creaking language of the reeds...

This is the here and now of our transit
the exploration of exploding seconds
a whisper of light through the crack of a closing door
in which you - yes, you - suddenly glimpse as it closes
the blue iridescent flame of a kingfisher

who - too fast for this passage of words - beak, feather,
bone, skull - moves quick and sudden as thought
between the elements that connect us;
and this bird that you thought you saw him see
was the bird and the thought that set him free.

3. rising & return

He left the boat at a leafy junction
just up from the spot where (fifty years since)
a rogue loco had fallen from a bridge
and jammed the slow flow of black country coal
along the cut's clay vein to the makers
of the nation's naval chain, and he followed
the path beside the southern spur, a quiet rising
of land and locks past where, in his lifetime,

a racecourse and public space - playing fields,
dens, rope swings and a school's nature trail -
had been surrounded by razor wire
and parcelled up into developers' lots
and flogged off as an all weather track
franchised to a betting syndicate,
two private estates, a retail park,
and, of course, a creche for working mums

and some boys in hoods on mountain bikes
chased a fat kid down the towpath
shouting stuff that proved (at least to them)
that what they sometimes feared they were
they could never possibly be - for they
were no one's fucking bitch, and they were alive,
and they were free - while around a bench
their paramours squabbled over coke and crisps
and wanting to share the bliss of the moment
texted, tweeted and twittered their love
ecstatic and dumb as hedgerow birds

and at the brow of the hill with the armatures
of commerce and industry spread beneath him
he rested between strangers at the roadside

one playing fiddle for the shrapnel
tossed into his upturned case, the other
drinking cider and squinting at the sun

and as he sat and waited for a ride
back to the place he had left behind
he laughed and closed his eyes and imagined
a dream in which I walked in peace through your head
and we were some of us living, some of us dead
and the city like dust on the wind blew past us.

carlisle

Between the trees
in the still lawns and quiet gardens,
between the factories, their chimneys,
the cobbled streets, the cathedral and the weir
ghosts walk. Romans and Reivers,
rich merchants, their servants,
their sons and daughters,
skivvies, navvies, soldiers, slaves
and mercenaries of empires now long gone
- in the breeze that blows in the grass
between flagstones, their voices echo on.

Each life is a shout on the earth
beneath the tree that gives us shelter.

The roof of each mouth is a church roof
and each tongue shapes our shared story.

And as each word, each step, each brick is laid,
each day, slowly, before our eyes, our city is remade.

carlisle - summer - foot & mouth

The dead man's voice carries on the wind
while outside the city this year's grass grows
this year's birds sing this year's flowers
bloom etcetera

but this time round the deal is different
as all around the county sickness
and economics empty the fields.

Spring passes in a wet
waxy paste of smoke
and summer burns larger still
the hole in our common sense

while somewhere
always somewhere
always somewhere else

death rattles down a windpipe
like an empty wellington tugged
from the sucking mud

while here, always here,
always here and now,
a mother with skin like curdled milk
pushes a buggy home from happy hour in the sunshine
and a kid who thinks a cow a comic cartoon mystery
and not a construct of blood, bone and money
walks behind her with Spiderman
on his t-shirt and tugs her hand
and wails for space dust until she cracks
and slaps him as a boy racer's dump valve coughs
and Bob Marley repeats the question:
"Is this love? Is this love that I'm feeling?"

between the buildings

Flames tear skyward from an oil drum
while each surrounding face projects
tiny, separate blazing landscapes
on snapping sticks, tattered news and rags.

Hands held palm open to the heat
mirror one another across the flicker
of dancing sparks and warmth - like a memory -
holds them for a moment in unstable community.

Ringed by a wall of rusted smoke-black steel
this impossible imagined land blazes
- implacably consumed by the absence
and loss which gave it birth. Embers hiss.
Rain spatters faces as they dissolve into dark.

Voices shout. Glass breaks. Footsteps echo.
People scream, or sigh, or laugh, or weep
or curl up in the city's fitful womb
of sleep and dream all manner of scary shit
- monsters, families, god knows what else -
while an older and more sober dream in which
shelter and commonality were sunk
corrupts to commodities, a pandered junk
traded between buildings ablaze with light.

he went down to the weir this morning

He went down to the weir this morning
his elbows brushing through the old man's beard,
and on top of its arc the summer's rubbish
was caught - a single shoe, white sole,
canvas upper, and a fencepost on the cusp
of falling water - waiting for the first
autumn storm to take them. The water
is bright and icy now, still glints like chrome
beneath a pale dome of sky. Muscovy ducks
sit on stones. Butterflies, autumn burnished, are blown
like fallen leaves. A new term beckons.
New challenges, new chores. And at their finish
when nights have drawn in and the tv chatters its trash
he pictures himself staring at the vodka bottle
and tries to laugh at the absurdity
of a word like alone. A single tiny glint
of fish skitters, blind and furious against the current
and rain falls into the upturned faces
of the bristling fields like answered prayers
or a half heard whisper in the water's roar.

waiting by the weir

Below the cathedral, above the weir,
in a brick house on a cobbled street where
insight, raw and tender as sex, flickers
through the words of the language spoken there,
he waits for her to come. He waits to hear
at the heart of their tongue an art and sense
that whispers; - let desire annihilate difference,
steal separate breath, the rented space between us,
birth and death; - let all collapse to nothing
and disappear. Let it leave two as one
and one as none or no more than the wink
of a seashell on the slope of a beach
washed by the edge of the tide's suck and reach
and while trees make waves in the paving stones
and cathedral bells beat like birds on the roofs
and jewels of smashed glass glint in the dumb light
of billboards that marry glamour to money
and gulls shriek their sudden prayers to the sky,
let the entwined elements - sea, air and sand -
caress where you lie on this wet lip of land,
let them bathe you, dry you, empty you, fill you,
fill up your emptiness, sweep you away.

Maybe later, asleep in each other's arms,
they dream of fish with rainbows in their scales
while, beyond the grid of streets and squares
through which, beneath a frozen arc of stars, a drunk
wanders, seeking passage home, the river flows
and fish - not dreamed, as real as you or I -
navigate its dark vibrating sinews
through echo and eddy, impelled by a pulse
in their blood as steady, cold and endless
as the moonlit water crossing the weir.
They have their course already charted.
They flicker and dart. They swim till they die,
the same way sparks swim a flame to the sky.

He waits for what has happened to happen again.
He waits for the gifts her presence can bring.
But in her absence he can only sing.

pictures of the gypsy kids

They lived by the cut and, when we passed by,
hitched a ride down the locks with my wife
and I. They brought a pet jackdaw they'd taught
a few words which it crowed while its feathers
creaked and its dull black beak knifed and prodded
the soil for seeds in the windowboxes
on our narrowboat roof as it descended
      the long,
           leaking
               flights
                  that lead   to the river.

"Oh, Mr! Oh, Mrs! We love your garden,"
the gypsy kids called as they steered
Kingfisher
a straight
          simple
              course between
                    gates
while my wife and I kept pace on the bank
and, with windlass and ratchet, worked the
                  boat
                  down.

The kids, like their bird, spoke words they couldn't see,
yet we watched through the glass as they leafed
through the books in our cabin, searching
impatiently for pictures to fissure
the blank walls of text and unlock their tales.

So they paused excitedly at photos,
drawings and diagrams and examined
butterflies, engines, a shire horse, a knot,
a quayside crane and a yacht - both brand new
one slate grey day now a century old -

and laughed with the raw wonder of recognition.

Tired of the language of books,
one kid picked up a metal box and shook
it close to his ear, eyes focussed inward,
as if intent on the metre and sense
of a poem composed by accident,
while a lass, made bolder by our absence,
kept watch for him over her shoulder.
Meanwhile, her friends picked and rummaged
through our galley and found fruit and spices,
candles, matches, fuses and money
while we looked away to make them think
we hadn't seen; but they knew that we had.

Later, where the canal met the river,
we stepped back aboard and, putting the kids
ashore from our berth between the dark, wet
stones of the last lock,

                    we   sailed   out

                                                              into

sunlight

               and the broad
                    flat   ambling
                                                  stretch of
                              the
                                        Severn
                                        which

                              eddied
                    and swirled
                              between
wharf and warehouse   and far wooded bank.

Seeing us go, the gypsy kids shouted
and waved, then whistled their jackdaw.
Cocking its head at their summons, the bird
skimmed across the expanding reach of light
between us and, perhaps, took with him,
gritty seed at the heart

of a ripened berry in his beak,
this thought:

that a while back, maybe a mile or two,
we'd been no more than neighbours, contiguous
as land is to water, earth to sky,
and our separate worlds had only meshed
as cogs do when cog drives neighbouring cog,
but then, as the kids explored the limits
of our tolerance the cupboards of our boat,
our boundaries seemed to dissolve until
we were submerged in a confluence of streams
and breathed the air of each other's dreams.

"Oh, Mr. Oh, Mrs, take us with you.
Oh, Mrs. We love your garden too,"
cried the kids. But they, being kids,
were kidding. And we, of course, knew.

                              Even so,
having touched everything, taken nothing,
they had forced us to join them in
their haphazard enquiry into
metaphysics and our shared nature.
More wild, wordless challenge than enquiry,
it issued from an imagination that,
however untutored, knew where it stood,
and a soul that, wherever that was,
felt at ease there. And this was the kingdom
of the gypsy kids, a land where the unbroken earth
bore flames, families, diesel, rivers, rust,
stripped engines, skinned rabbits, flowers, blood
and a trust wrought and teased till it was hard
as iron, sharp as flint, bright and sudden
as a reflected glint in the dark jewel
of a jackdaw's eye.

                    We're shorebound now,
fixed fast in marriage as tight clasped hands,

yet as we walk together to the place where
all roads and ditches and memories end,
I still hear, like wind in the branches
of a bare tree on the brow of a hill,
the faint, distant voices of children
calling across the water.

"Oh, Mister. Oh, Missus, come back."

what he sees when he looks at her

He says it is the face of many races
and the palace built in all our blood,
words copped from Robert Hunter and the Dead,
that show his age and the generations
between them - (she likes the intricacy
of hip hop, the dialectic of rap, was born
to shop) - yet each time he sees her
they unwrap themselves in his memory
and remind him of the shy, reckless grace
with which she unwraps herself for him.

Sometimes, where world and sunshine meet,
by terraces, schools and small shops,
past factories, agriculture
and their detritus, they walk together
beside a broad stream and the laughter
of light's fragmented dance on its surface,
and where the water churns and falls
across a weir's arc and the local
folk have built a ladder for the fish,
some, tiny as dreams, swim round the boulders
of their toes as they stir clouds in the silt,
and once he spilt the river's endless being
across her breasts and asked of her, asked anyone
and anything, the shadow dappled fence,
the dusty path, the sky's benign indifference,
the lowing cows, the wind in the grasses,

"Tell me, this hot stuff that steams up the glasses,
this ancient illness that cooks up the brain,
that touches us once and leaves us insane;
tell me. Please. Are you sure? Is there no cure?"

Wind blows. Grass bends. Wind blows. Nothing ends.
She smiles, presses her head in his shoulder.
The river flows on. They both grow older.

Flight

oxford road

Yesterday, years ago, tomorrow and today
- go with this collapse of time it's part of the joke -
this bloke comes out of a library and meets a tramp
propped up against the wall where Oxford Street
ends in St Peter's Square. Tramp - piss soaked
weather stained, with the usual vacant stare -
lifts his finger skywards and says:
If God's looking down from somewhere up there
he'd see that this library rotunda
looks no different from a merry go round
but with books - not painted horses - kept inside.
Know what I mean, mate?

So, tramp takes a suck at his smackinacan
while man thinks: Wait. Don't wait.
Keep your head on straight.
Don't walk. Walk. Follow your feet.
Then he ricochets off down the street
like someone spun dizzy from a machine
at a fairground or someone just for fun
shot from the rifled barrel of a gun
and with a clutch of books beneath his arm
he wonders just what time it is - and what day -
just as you may wonder what page we're on,
where we're going with this, what year we're in,
and what age the man is. So, first of all:

he's a young man, not much more than a boy
- amongst the borrowed books is - just published -
His Toy, His Dream, His Rest which in time
he will grow to know & love & find (repeatedly)
dreamsongs 90 & 265 echo in his mind (repeatedly)…
…anyway, this young man - to tell the truth -
is partly me; and if it's true that I am you
and you are me then we are partly like those three
blokes, who at this point are new to this tale -

- an Englishman, an Irishman and...no...
...a Mancunian, an Aussie, and a guy from Guyana -
who we see walk into this bar on a street round the corner
from the Classic which is screening a double bill
(*Giant* and *Persona*) just down from The Palace
where, two years from now - or has this time
already been? - Lowell George - soon to be dead
or is this only a dream? - at a sound check for Little Feat
will sing *Willing* to rows of empty seats.

But that's just by the bye, let's focus in:
- the guy from Guyana is China Jimmy
and he knows Farokh Engineer, while the Manc just wants
to flog the Aussie two tickets to the cricket
and our man with the books, unnoticed, passes on
- not hard, by the way, since he doesn't exist
being just a desperado, a gorilla in your mist,
an organisation of matter, a narrative trope
to move the tale from A to B to C.
He's a matchstick man on which I hang a hat,
he hangs a coat and we hang our tattered dreams -
but go along with it. The fact that all of us
can be represented by a single man
- a pilgrim Everyman unstuck in time and space
with his head - in truth - all over the place -
is also part of the joke. So watch him
at Charles Street smile at a kid in a queue
and wonder where his road will lead to.

Will he meet cute with his happy ever after,
then, years later, share the cliché and the laughter
as he tells the tale to contented friends
of how running to class, late for the sky,
they collided, spilled books in the street
- *Cat's Cradle, Bird Lives! The Drawings of Paul Klee,
Tender is the Night, Decline and Fall, Smallcreep's Day*
and as they knelt down, felt glances meet
and in that fleeting instant - both knew?

In another lifetime that might turn out true
but not today when, crossing against the traffic,
he doesn't even know what tomorrow holds...
that, stood on the steps of The Deaf Institute
while a flakey headed drunk shakes his fist
at the rain rammed dark and light polluted sky
above the pulsing artery of Oxford Road,
he will sense the seasons in his bones and skin
and suddenly, clearly and forever know
that however strong should be our need to go
no road, no side street, no footpath or line of desire
can ever take us home. This - of course - is hardly news
but because time makes sure that no one goes
to the same place more than once - he will pick
and pick and pick at the only thread we know
- the one that binds us to the dead and to each other -
until every image - the fields at dusk in which he walked,
some old street of dreams down which you zoom and fly,
this world in which we live and grow and, grown, begin to die -
will some day fade to a whispered word
a murmur of light caught in a closing eye
the path of a cloud or a bird and then
an empty sky against which something still
will knock, still knocks, is endlessly knocking
- a child's imagination, a branch on a door,
a wooden wheel creaking across a floor,
an old man's cane, the steps of a dancer -
and because it is our nature to want to know
he'll ask who's there but get no answer.

sonnet for macsweeney

Accept it. The bottle's empty, the teat
turned inside out. Your slurred, milky phoneline
flannel has gone for good. You've crossed the Tyne
to buy a Barca shirt and big stand seat
with Homer (Simpson, of course) and Ed Dorn.
Apollinaire's there too. He wants to dance
and knock back drinks; - cocktails of petulance,
guile, erudition, wit and a stubborn
volatile spirit that gives the mix its kick.
Will you brave it again? Let your shaking hands
steer unconditional love's demands
toward one more drunken head-on smash? The brick
wall and bottle wait, and the lesson no one learns:
- give up nothing, something gives. Learn or crash and burn.

highway child

Some people may call him a tramp
but you know it goes a little deeper than that…

after Jimi Hendrix

1. short story

Chas, my brother, told stories and he drank.
These facts were his double helix, coded
Coils of ancient cellular memory
That would not be denied. They made his life.

An original and creative man,
A funny and uncompromising soul,
A cliché too, an alcoholic hack,
A shaman breathing spirits in the air
To quicken and spark the slow daily drudge
Of making meaning - dull, fastidious
And eventually impossible work -
He took to the bottle with a vengeance.

2. the premise

I whisper this, but they say, that nameless
They who we always say are saying things,
That human life is an experiment.
Charmed, belligerently cracked, or just
The cautious dipping of a toe or two
Into the stream of freaky collisions
That make up the world as they go along,
Its outcome unknown, its method suspect,
Word has it that its subject is ourselves.

1990: I am round at your house
And the mad scientist on the tv

In a cartoon for kids you watch daily
Mixes chemicals in his secret lab
And rants about power and ruling the world.
You pour and swallow, pour again and smirk
At his stupidity. No kids' stuff this.
You are deep in your experiments
With alcohol and space-time. Your living
Room is your laboratory and you've learned
How to disappear. Soon you will be gone.

3. first voices

You heard voices. You saw things. It was funny
At first. You lay hungover in your bed
While children fired rockets at your windows
Screaming, "Scrooge! Scrooge! Scrooge!"
                                    Or maybe not,
Although no one could make you believe it.

Why should you? It happened to you, not them.
A possibility not countenanced
Was that kids, rockets, screams - all but the bed
And the window - were insubstantial,
Imagined not by you, but by liquor.

4. unrequited love

The liquor you lied you could take or leave
Was your lover. But with no kids, dad dead,
Your wife in a wreck, smashed sideways then cut
From her car in a coma, relationships changed.

D, when she woke, was different. Sharp lawyers
Chased her ambulance, waved shrouds, made bedside
Hay from trauma. Cash might heal her, they said,
And you couldn't, or wouldn't, say different.

Desperate, you turned instead to the lover
Whose whispers darkened your senses and dreams.
"Renounce nothing," they said. "You need not grieve;
For that which does not kill you makes you strong."

What crap. The voices were yours. Grief is only
Love's unsettled scores. Your lover had no need
To take or leave, no need at all for you.

5. how it seemed

In a dingy home with broken appliances,
And walls discoloured by nicotined breath,
You let yourself go. Your armchair grew stained
With misuse. Your clothes grew cigarette burns.
Inside them your body weighed less than a child's,
While your cat, the house's passive smoker,
Scratched at the carpet's damp sugar of booze.

And then worse:
you'd sit till dawn beside your busted gramophone and
unravelled tapes,
your spidery hand raving through notebooks and unsent
letters about the assholes who persecuted you
or left you alone to shout tormented defiance at those
voices - or maybe the silence - that said,
"Get help. This cannot continue."

6. september 1991

God knows what those last days were like for D
Before she phoned and said you were ill.
Though not entirely unexpected news,
It shocked me still. You said you'd drink yourself
To death if people came and interfered.
Some threat. What was the plan if we didn't?

You slept on the ward whilst the trees shut down
Their yearly systems outside your window.
The programme copied in ten billion leaves
Decayed in the rain. You were cut and drained
And put on a machine. Eventually
They switched you off. For days each fallen leaf
Seemed singular; - windblown granite flaking
From the edifice of your last summer.

7. two beaches

.............young men, loose change: 1968

Evening, our youthful, angry minds unhinged
By dope, we drink and exult in the world.
We walk and our hands shuttle a bottle
Beside the crab high phosphorescent surf
And moon tugged tide. We're arguing, laughing,
Discussing the system, and you describe
Its workings thus:
              There are two fat spiders
In a bath. One trapped frantic at the foot
Of the tub's white walls, one waiting hidden
In the tap. Just pull the plug, you said,
Why should we choose between these intruders?

From Street Hawk Annual 1986

"Venice California: 2.38 pm.
The fresh sea breezes mingle with bizarre
aromatic cocktails of coconut
suntan lotion, frying onions, burning
rubber and cordite. For once the Beach Park's
carefree amateur circus of freaks,
acrobats, weightlifters, clowns, and jugglers
has packed up its psychological tent
and closed down the show.

Elaborate picnics lie uneaten on the sand."

For my brother: January 1949 - September 1991

english ghost dance

Though you've gone to join the endless dead
I carry you still encoded in my head
& from the broken signs that strew
our English reservation pick a few
last questions - leaves in the wind - to stir you.

So: did you burn the tickets to the rock & roll show
& leave Liverpool docks black & smouldering in a dream?
Did you overturn buses, bottle fire & torch the arcades?
Did you put cats, sleeping in the sunshine,
on the white rooftops of Andalusia?

Were you sleeping off your Sunday lunch
or walking Westmorland's wooded hills with your notebook
in search of a fox, a falling leaf, a broken oar?
When did you work your magic on the signposts?

Was it you turned every journey into the road home
& the road home into a mathematical equation,
a comic strip, a fire viewed from a train window,
a balloon escaping, a child left speechless?

Was it you who wrote this while I slept?
Did you sneakypete my darkened rooms
& just now fabricate order there?

Just then. Leaving once again. Was that you?

dad's end of the deal

TO MY FIRSTBORN (William)

What can I say to you
Who wasn't here long enough
To know (in anything but the most
Rudimentary abstractions) love? Without
Comparisons, how could you ever tell
That being loved was better than
Not being loved? You never
Even knew what it was to
Be held, or smiled at,
Or kissed, either
In greeting or
Goodbye.

So I say to you now what you once told me
That life is shrouded in painful mystery.

TO MY SECONDBORN (Jack)

First, do not expect apology.
Because I fear that in your young, angry eyes
The world with its training schemes,
Shit jobs, stupid adults and human music
Of heartbreak, divorce and baby come back
Must already seem, beside the accelerated
Forkings of the myriad roads of possibility,
Old hat and pitifully weary, I apologise
Already more often than I ought. You,
You see, like me, like she, like he,
Like we, have been given this fine
Flawed gift we can never repay.
So spend it in wonder and
Wonder first at this:
What if you had a son? What if you did
And he died, never touched by the hands

Never held by the arms of the woman
Or man who made him? What then?
Would rage rip up the glossy stillborn
Sentimental dreams of domesticity
On which we gorge our hungry hearts?
Would every passing hour become a question
stripped stark and bare as a winter tree
Or a child laid three brief days on his back
Being fed air that, eventually, forgive me,
I begin to lose the thread of this or the point
- it distresses me still - he no longer wanted to breathe?

If you will try to understand these things
Then I, as usual, will thank you for your
Kindness and patience, fine qualities both.
Give me a harder time than I feel I deserve
And I, as usual, as you would to me, will say to you:
"Fuck off."

For life is barbed by truth's painful stories.

THIRDBORN (Sam)

Where is your pen? Where are your shoes?
Or your passport? Or the money for your lunch?
Or the note that says you have lost these things
But should be humoured? It seems sometimes that
Your forgetfulness is a search for an escape from things
You find tedious and, in choosing this path, you have
Discovered a tunnel that leads back to a deep lost continent
Of dreams, where lion and lamb, weary of waiting for the day
They will lie down together, have decided instead
To make common cause with the dolphins.

I remember seventeen years since
On a surf rumbling Pembrokeshire beach
Beneath a tumbling cathedral of clouds
Remade as streaming pennants in the wind
You sat for hours while the sun burned your back

And your eyes traced the shape of a seashell
Held in your hand. Because you choose to lose yourself
In such wonder, I do more than humour your quiet humour,
I honour it. Still, as parent, for some years yet,
I am honour bound to ask: this road you have chosen
Like the elegant spiral of the shell that leads from its
Sculpted frozen lip inward, back through ever tighter coiled
Time to the moment that saw it first created,
Where does it end? And if we ever get there
Do you think we'll need shoes?

Amongst the world's seductive whispers let me say:
It takes a kind of forthright guile to answer complex questions
with a smile.

FOURTHBORN (Tom)

And then you, son, the one I won, in a raffle,
The way you, having lost a dad you never knew,
Won me instead. A double headed twist of fate.
As deals go, from my side, it's been not too bad
but tell me true, how's it been for you?

Remember that Christmas?
That white Christmas? How corny
Could it get? Big fat white flakes fell all night
And now, on Christmas day, I want to stay
Indoors and drink Spar Scotch and watch
Indiana Jones and his dad, while you,

As kids do when it snows, want to go out and play
And when you ask I push you away
And think: "Yes, I know it's Christmas,
But Jesus Christ it's cold out!"

But your persistence as usual wins the day
And while a bun turns in your mother's oven
We take the secondborn son's sledge to a high white hill
And under a sky, icy and grey,

I push you again, and you fly away.

FIFTHBORN (Lily)

I fear, dear daughter, that here,
Even after you phone me from a festival
To tell me the Red Hot Chillies are on
And do I want to listen and next
you're off to the silent rave in the silent rave tent
And despite the fact that I, diminished
Daily by age, illness and a shot memory,
Rave silently at the silence that makes everyone
The butt of the world's joke…

Even after all this I fear that here
The rough hewn sinew of these arguments
Becomes just the ditty
Of a besotted dad who walks through the sad
Soft rain that falls on us all and thinks:
Very pretty
Very clever
Spoilt rotten
Loved forever
Will I ever
Will I never
Tell you a truth that was once told me
- that life is shrouded in painful mystery?

don't cry

Pets, parents, children, friends
go the same way as strangers
in the end. Mice, men, the best
laid plans all die. Don't cry.
Keep busy and give thanks.

When the tale that links each heartbeat
to the last starts to unravel
in the haywire scribble and bleep
of monitors, when we rise up
and wander the maze of hospital
corridors, looking for the door
that let us in and find instead
god only knows what... Come near.
Help us join dot to last dot.
Whisper the words we need to hear.

And when we're gone, like I am gone,
ashes scattered and chatter chatted
amongst kindness, canapés and wreaths,
brush the dust from your shoe and go. Leave us
to blow and leach amongst beech trees, roots and rain
and know these words are true: I love you.

Okay. It's said. Now, since you're still here
go sort things out. The spirits were clear.
The wine was green. Brown was the beer.
It did not kill you, all the drink you drank.
You are not at peace. You are not content.
Instead you are happy. Give thanks.

Oct 2005, for my mum

learning to look

1. late show

"Funerals are pretty compared to deaths,"
Blanche tells her sister Stella in *Streetcar.*
Who would argue? To comfort the living
We surround life's empty husk with ritual.

In some places, firecrackers and drums
Clap and dance their racket round the casket
To scare off evil spirits. In others,
Mortal remains are floated down rivers,
Set on fire, or talon-hooked and beak-ripped
Apart, carried to the world's four corners
By sacred birds to feed their crag-bound young.

Here, a man in the family business
Brushes his sleeve and asks which we'd prefer:
Should we cremate or inter? His chair creaks.
His solicitude suffocates and we forget:
A funeral's a way of setting us free.
At least it used to be. Now some new riff
Twists common sense and decency skewiff,
Exposing the weakness in these old tales.

2. an interrupted process

My mum had a younger brother called Max.
She said that when her parents buried him
(Only thirty and dead in a car crash)
They lost the coffin at some traffic lights.

From a paybox in a pub mum phoned round
To find out where the body had gone to.
Meanwhile my grandparents - both in a state
As you can imagine, as you'd be too -

Sat stricken and bewildered in the snug,
Failing to see the funny side of things.

Maybe if they were living now they would.
This was a mishap after all, a fluke,
A macabre twist in grief's bleak procession.

They were streetwise enough to know these things
Happen, that things could've been plenty worse.
They could have found no wood for a casket,
No fuel for the hearse, the cemetery closed
Or sown with mines, the mourners killed for sport.

3. channel surfing

Been there. Seen that. See it again. Smuggled
Huddled in a chattering trash of signs,
From ended life to edited tape, from tape
To screen to mind, the half departed dead
Return and return, whispering languages
We never learned to learn. Poised to blink they
Mutilate text delete blink erase and
So on and so on, until the process
Is complete, before you even know it.

4. wildlife

Stories have threads that tugged too often break,
That woven make strong cloth. One channel shows
A family of hyenas feeding
On carrion, bloodied heads burrowing
Through bowels and shattered carcass. Another
Serves up, let's say, images of orca,
Black, white and grey, like snow on a mountain
Or blood burned dry on a sun bleached stone,
Its ton weight surging through the breaking surf
To steal a pup seal from the pebbled shore

And in its icy, elemental space,
Feeding a hunger deeper than hunger,
Kill it. Meanwhile, safe in my element,
I look and, so as not to look, learn tricks.

This is just nature - how it always is.
Its savage, beautiful balance demands
I do nothing. Real action's not in the world
Anyway, but in the eye, in seeing.

A bird, the colour of a gun, chatters.
The story's the same, we've heard it before.
The thread breaks, the cloth slowly unravels.
The lion does not lie down with the lamb.

5. fairytale

How did we get here?
What's being buried?
For whom do we grieve?
Why can't we find them?
Where must we go next?

The world is full of noise.
Our children are lost and hungry in the woods.
It is getting dark.

possible futures: number 70

As they walk, clasping hands,
through city streets in winter light,
a wind tattered fragment of music
blows through their unclasped minds,
chased beyond hearing in sinuous shapes
that twist beneath the cold blue sky
like pages blown from a newspaper
without a date.

Later their entwined fingers
will separate and scatter
new tunes like sun across their skin,
and tomorrow her body's warmth
will be smeared like printer's ink
across his eyes and fingertips,
and she will taste him still on her breath
as they escape even memory and bask
like benevolent alligators
on the smashed stone steps of a courthouse
in a long forgotten country.

poem for my wife

Soon they will say goodbye for the last time
but, for now, they skirt the perimeters
of their shared ecology. Birds migrate
southward and leave heartbeats in her blue breast.
She feels sun in the structures and hollows

of her bones. The porous rainclouds are wet
on her lip as she bites. We live, she and he
(her and me), in a town where rules are soon
to be suspended. We read the signs we need.

In the kids' pictures tacked to the fridge
stands a painted, nameless, numberless house
with gate, fence and path, tree, stream and bridge,
- a place where beasts are transformed by love.

He would solve her riddles, return favours for her
if he could, seek amongst strangers a saviour,
mild and implacable as the rise and fall of the tide,
to cherish and nurture her when he is gone.

Folk fall out. They fall out of her sky.
She populates the land between them
with quirks and whispers. The dark of her eye
reflects back street signs as burnished texts,
asymmetric palindromes that map the weave
and frayed, unravelling hem of the world.

Love, lose, solve, evolve. Do this, or die.

We burrow blindly to this edge alone
but turn back together: - from the icy wheel of stars
to the ache of weather & light, the steel
in the blade of grass, the mark of sleek
cubs' pawprints on the cold, white door.

once upon a time in cumberland

He remembers now
his memory tense, bunched like a fist,
how by the flower stall in the market
back in 1956 - or was it yesterday -
the skin of his wrist brushed her cuff
and it was enough

and how in August out west
they lay amongst the fireweed and the foxgloves
in the ragged grass across the river
from where the clatter and wheeze
of the steelworks trucks
and the hoarse quacked laughter
of the estuary ducks rang in the air
and how she kissed him and he kissed her
and he kissed her again
in August out west and then

how because they were young all the rest
of it fell quite perfectly into place
- the sunlit room adrift in space
her words on the mirror her breath on his face
the children's voices in a distant street
the creak of a floorboard beneath her feet -

and he felt then and knows now
- as he stands by the flower stall
in the market - today, not yesterday, not 1956 -
that all of these things are one thing
- fist, flame, flower, hand, heat, heart -
that folds moments into memories then
unfurls them in the world again.

ferry

she sleeps beside him on a seat
as he, sleepy too,
half high on the high sea,
haunted by ghosts,
caught between longings,
stretched between coasts,
wonders how he can tell her
how much he loves her

while outside in the weather
gulls' wings beat moonbeams
into the metal sky and the ship's wake
disappears into the darkness
from which they have come

for a doctor on retirement

Not long after my brother died
I saw, then tore from a Sunday paper, this:

"Ognuno sta solo sul cuor della terra
traffito da un raggio di sole:
ed e subito sera."

It was written by a Sicilian and translated thus:

"Each of us is alone on the heart of the earth,
pierced by a ray of sun:
and suddenly it's evening."

A doctor retiring. Some joke.
Might as well ask a writer to quit
or a painter to donate his brushes
to the bin man. Society's shaped
by our inescapable nature - red
in tooth and claw, shot through
with quirky mercy - and life
is no more than the breath
it takes to breathe it
in, to hold it, then
breathe out again.

poem for george tod

Between each evening's glimmer,
each dawn's murmur and gleam,
we are islands, families of clustered light
in a dark, unrelenting stream
where, in the stillness, in the wind,
in each river's endless change,
everything must come, unremembered,
to nothing. Yet you visit me.
Like the taste on my lips
or the seed of a smile,
you visit me still.

Sometimes,
when the creak of the walking wheel
ceases for a second beneath a willow's
wooden lightning, and the flutter
of silence and the pattern of leaves
pass like metamorphosed shadow through
the whirling ruin of sense and memory
that is my every last day, I still
see clearly, still say what I see,
still make jokes, speak truth,
still.

I have grown angry, grown weary
of anger, given up weariness,
chosen rest. Bound no longer
by the impossible clauses and demands
of life's contract, I have torn it up,
fired advisors, and taken
to the clouds. I unravel
into the laughter of children,
while work, like a shoelace,
comes undone, and the world,
like a pun, like a metaphor,
like a play in words, like my bed

every morning, is unmade.

When you no longer visit me,
when these hands no longer wander
across this unmade map of sheets,
when you are safe once more in your certainties
with what passes for order restored,
I will cease to be what I have become,
- unruly impulse wired into unfettered dream -
and I will be instead something calmer and better,
a murmur of light that gives shape to your memories,
a guide to those lost in the stream.

changes

Things grow in silence;
a smear of smoke climbing
from chimney to sky,
a wave before it breaks,
a plant's germination in cold earth;
the world's improvised forms
give shape to unmeasured time.

Light strikes the anvil
of a cloud and sootflecks
from an imagined furnace
blow across the pale orange
yolk of an autumn sun.

As they veer through the air
these dark seeds on the wind
turn to birds, and each wingbeat,
a moment's captured light,
turns birds to jagged pearls
whose torn strings swirl and swing
between earth and darkening sky.

In what seems almost to be
an impossibility,
wind weaves these broken threads
into a spangled cape
of starlings and drapes it
through a tangle of branches,
that is map, record and witness
to the unremembered work
of days and leaves and birds,
and as raindrops speckle
the dusty palms of fields,
bare trees turn to torches,
ablaze with mindless song.

tiny prayer

when
burned out
white bones turn
heavy & cold & brittle

&
each fast
retreating second
splits into all
the rest

&
meanwhile
earth winds through
love's everlasting blueprint of days
like dog roses wind
through a windy
hedgerow

&
across the city streets
& chalked & broken flags &
brick red faces

&
memories
& stories & dreams &
all these things

forever

help us all
keep intact

anything
we wish

the colour of birds

Home from work, bone tired, one afternoon in autumn,
I scattered seed on the keys and summoned the birds.
Soon, tapping their beaks - just like I'd taught them -
against the pane, they were gathered on the ledge
and I rose from my table to let them in.

Black, green, green-black, yellow-flecked and red,
their lyric colour-song of feathers said
to flutter, follow and take flight
through darkening sky and dying light
but I did not go.

I waited instead for a sign, an accident,
a collision of sense and moment, an omen
sent to help invent, or reinvent more bearably, the world
through which we foraged, the birds and I, but none came
- only steps on stones and chalk on flags,
a child's hopscotch outside in the street,
echoing from what I was to hopes I could not meet -
as yellow beaks scavenged among the keys.

Now, with the birds gone, I hunt and peck at memory,
recalling how their presence brought me rest,
how from caws and cries and stolen scraps and silence,
their urgent, mindless music wove a nest.

the transparency of shadows

they say that they said

that round the fires in this shanty people have heard
I have ripped up all written records of the where and when
and now must rest trust in all too fallible memory

but I have also heard said that the souls of the dead
can enter the unfortunate (or otherwise)
souls of the living to nourish and instruct them

and someone with a name now long gone from me
once claimed literature was a whisper from within
sent on its way by a symbolic system of myth
and that this was how myths within men
will think and live on unbeknownst to them

and I have read or heard said
that eagle and rock are made from one thing
transparent as a shadow cast on wind shaped waves

and though I've been told we hold all our days
in our bones and that lines on paper thin skin
can trace paths back through exhausted folds of light
to the mysterious absence at the labyrinth's heart
it has begun to feel to me as if all around us
our maps and mazes and our diagrams and charts
- all of them - have begun to swim and burn

and since I know that looking too hard for a thing
can only increase the disorder in which it is hidden
I pass on hand to hand only this
- whether legend or fact I don't know -
that on long voyages Vikings would take ravens
that they kept in cages and then let fly free
and if - or when - they did not return
it was there they believed land would be.